# A

# WORTHY

# EXPERIENCE

Script by
John Sheridan Thomas

April 15, 2015

# PREFACE

A WORTHY EXPERIENCE is about economics and national economic policy. It is presented in a fictional setting - a seminar consisting of conversations among an economics professor and her students probing the sources of wealth creation and how government policies impact on the economy.

This subject should be of great concern to everyone. Over the past seven years, median household income across the nation declined $5,000. Even worse, it has been in decline since 1999, even though the Gross Domestic Product (GDP) continues to rise.

What policies promote growth? Conversely what policies stymie growth? This seminar addresses these questions, and suggests appropriate actions to unshackle our sluggish economy.

**Astro College
of
Science & Mathematics**

# ECONOMIC POLICY

# SEMINAR

**Participants**

**Professor Regina (Reggie) Worthy, PHD**

**Stu: Any student in a class of 25**

# LECTURES

# 1.  WEALTH CREATION

**Prof. Reggie:**  First we address the question of how wealth is created; that is the collective wealth of the nation and its citizens.  We are not concerned here with the attainment of individual wealth.

There are three primary contributors of wealth – natural resources, technology and productivity.  The human mind molds these three into economic enterprises that produce useful and then more useful goods and services for the people.

# Natural Resources

**Prof. Reggie:** The earth provides a multitude of resources: food and water from the lands and seas; minerals from the earth.

Through the ages we learned how to convert these natural resources into products that enhance our quality of life: feeding growing populations while vastly diminishing the physical effort needed to survive and prosper.

**Stu:** I'm sure glad we don't have to plow fields by hand any more.

**Prof. Reggie:** Arable land is one of the essential resources of life. The United States is most fortunate in having vast fertile lands, bathed in sunshine and rain; and equally blessed with mild climates. And we have an abundance of fossil fuels - coal, natural gas, and oil – to provide the needed energy.

**Stu:** Is this a global warming lecture?

**Prof. Reggie:** No, but it would be foolish to forgo the vast benefits of fossil fuels without just cause and adequate alternatives.

**Stu:** Well, what do natural resources have to do with economics?

**Prof. Reggie:** Most things of economic value are derived from the earth's resources.

**Stu:** I guess that's kinda obvious. Isn't it?

**Prof. Reggie:** It's not just fossil fuels; it's ores from which we derive metals (copper, iron, steel), and many other critical elements.

**Stu:** All things physical . . . and they sure don't come out of thin air!

**Prof. Reggie:** Nor do they come from space . . . at least not yet. Of course what we do with our natural resources depends on the state of technology at the time . . . perhaps I should add . . . and the political fashions of the moment.

**Stu:** Natural resources and politics - strange bedfellows.

# Technology

**Prof. Reggie:**  We convert natural resources into usable products through technology.  Take communications for example.  In little more than 100 years we progressed from the pony express to an instant internet.

**Stu:**  Pony express!  Ha, that's a laugh – linking a pony to an express.

**Prof. Reggie:**  Yours is a retrospective view.  Back when the pony express replaced the stage coach for mail delivery the time saved was quite impressive.  You see, it's all a matter of relativity.

**Stu:**  Ok.  And now we have Facebook.  That's a real technology revolution.

**Prof. Reggie:**  Please . . . Facebook is an app; internet is the technology.  We could recite example after example of economic gains derived from technology, but we'll settle for just one here.

**Prof. Reggie:** I like to think of the cotton gin as an icon of technology advancement. It was such a simple mechanical device, but one that had immense economic consequences.

**Stu:** How so?

**Prof. Reggie:** Shortly after graduating from Yale, Eli Whitney invented a mechanical device to separate seeds from cotton. Essentially it was a filter powered by a Stanley steam engine. Whitney's cotton gin cleaned fifty times more cotton than one man by hand. Consequently over the next 17 years the cotton harvest grew from 180,000 pounds to 93 million pounds - a huge economic leap.

**Stu:** How about a bullet verses an arrow. That's really accelerating.

**Prof. Reggie:** Yes it is. And remember Henry Ford's Tin Lizzie? No, of course you don't. It was 100 years ago when the first mass-produced automobile was manufactured. Seemingly overnight the automobile was within the price range of everyman.

**Stu:** And we have risen from the Wright brothers 120 feet flight at Kitty Hawk to space rockets in just one century.

**Prof. Reggie:** Faster and higher! I believe we all get the point. Let's move on to the third component of wealth creation – productivity.

# Productivity

**Prof. Reggie:** No matter how automated our factories, people will have productive tasks to do. And the more productive we are, the more wealth we have to share.

**Stu:** Productivity . . . is that like work smarter, not harder?

**Prof. Reggie:** Let's not denigrate hard work. But yes it is the leverage we achieve through technology that pays off big. We organize the processes, build the machinery. We develop the technologies and invent the products. Then we produce and deliver the goods.

Human ingenuity is the driving force.

**Stu:** That takes brains!

**Prof. Reggie:** Yes; and every brain needs nurturing.

**Stu:** Nurturing! Is that what you're doing here?

**Prof. Reggie:** We are expanding your horizons and enhancing your economic worth.

**Stu:** Well, I surely hope you succeed at both.

**Prof. Reggie:** Of course you do.

## 2. THE ENABLER

**Prof. Reggie:** We considered three primary factors of economic advancement: natural resources, technology, and productivity. These are proactive ways to grow the economy and increase wealth provided government does not stymie these processes.

A productive economy needs a civil society within which to organize and produce. That is a primary role of government. It can facilitate wealth creation; it can squelch it. It can be an enabler; it can be a disabler.

**Stu:** Dr. Jeckel or Mr. Hyde!

**Prof. Reggie:** Our government provides civil and criminal laws to protect us and our property. It also provides a variety of common services that are more efficiently provided collectively than individually.

**Stu:** Such as?

**Prof. Reggie:** Public safety and education.

**Stu:** How about national defense and interstate highways.

**Prof. Reggie:** Yes. So you see government plays a critical role in the economy. It is one that requires a delicate balance; and that's not easy to get right. If government is too lax, "robber barons" rule. If government is too overbearing, initiative is stymied and the economy contracts.

We must not overlook the Constitution. Its protection of property rights is the bedrock of economic opportunity. That protection enables us to create and accumulate wealth.

**Stu:** Government can make or break the economy?

**Prof. Reggie:** Of course it can. To "make" the economy, that is to enable economic growth, we must govern ourselves with a light touch; avoiding excessive command and control from Washington.

**Stu:** Yea, abolish command and control!

**Prof. Reggie:** It is, of course, not that simple.

# 3. GROSS DOMESTIC PRODUCT

**Prof. Reggie:** The Gross Domestic Product, GDP for short, is the recognized measure of economic performance.

**Stu:** What does the GDP do?

**Prof. Reggie:** The GDP counts the total spending on goods and services – that is transactions within and between businesses, consumers and government.

**Stu:** When I spend money to see a basketball game, is that counted?

**Prof. Reggie:** The GDP counts four categories of spending.

- Personal consumption: This is what we spend our money on – goods and services.
- Private investments: This spending is on non-consumables such as buildings, manufacturing equipment, residential property, and intellectual property.
- Government spending at all levels – Local, state, and federal.
- Net exports.

**Prof. Reggie:** The cost of your basketball ticket is counted in the receipts of sporting events, and classified as personal consumption.

**Stu:** What does the GDP tell us?

**Prof. Reggie:** The GDP is widely employed to measure the nation's economic well being. Presumably a rising GDP is evidence of economic success.

**Stu:** Then a falling GDP is evidence of failure!

**Prof. Reggie:** Keynesian economists view a GDP decline as an economic downturn – that is a recession or depression.

There is a bit of circular logic involved in the GDP. Its construction pre-ordains that government spending "stimulates" the economy.

**Stu:** I sense that you are saying "stimulates the economy" with tongue-in-cheek. Do you really mean that?

**Prof. Reggie:** Excuse me. I should have said government spending stimulates the GDP.

**Stu:** So . . . ah . . . government spending, no matter what it is for, counts as much as say a company fracking for gas in Pennsylvania.

**Prof. Reggie:** Dollar-for-dollar they have the same impact on the GDP.

**Stu:** Same as the dollars my parents pay for my tuition?

**Prof. Reggie:** Ultimately your tuition is worth what you make of it; meanwhile the GDP assumes it is worth every dollar spent.

**Stu:** Well a dollar is a dollar; so what am I missing?

**Prof. Reggie:** You are missing three GDP shortcomings in measuring the health of the economy.  Here they are.

# Value of Purchases

**Prof. Reggie:** When you have $100 to spend, you have multiple products to choose from and multiple manufacturers of a given product. It is reasonable to assume that whatever you buy is worth the expenditure. Certainly it is to you.

On the other hand, most government purchases are mandated. Consequences vary: economic values of government purchases range from nil (symbolically represented by the "bridge to nowhere") to a whole dollar.

**Stu:** Government spenders are using someone else's money.

**Prof. Reggie:** Yes, in which case purchases may not have the same worth as when it is your own hard-earned money; or your parent's.

**Stu:** Gotcha! Government spends and the GDP goes up, irrespective of what the real economy does.

**Prof. Reggie:** Exactly.

## Costs of Regulations

**Prof. Reggie:**  The GDP does not account for the negative impact most regulations have on the economy.  In fact the GDP turns these costs up-side-down: costs of regulatory compliance go directly into the GDP as economic gains.

**Stu:**  How so?

**Prof. Reggie:**  Every company must sooner or later make a profit.  To do so it must include all costs when pricing its products.  When government imposes regulatory requirements on businesses, invariably those requirements add to their costs.

**Stu:**  And when corporate costs increase, prices increase, pushing the GDP up.

**Prof. Reggie:**  Exactly.

**Stu:** Prices go up – that's bad.  The GDP goes up – that's good.  Sounds like Abbot and Costello.

**Prof. Reggie:**  The prices we pay must include regulatory compliance costs.  But for the most part compliance does not increase the values of our purchases proportionally to the cost increases.

Why don't we just give everyone money, say a million dollars? End of problems - the GDP skyrockets.

**Prof. Reggie:** If you were very quick-footed, you might come out ahead. But you have to be at the front of the line at the handout window. Then you must quickly buy something physical like a mansion or an airplane, because within a few hours your million dollars would be worthless.

**Stu:** How about gold?

**Prof. Reggie:** Yes, that works too. But it's not nearly as exciting as owning an airplane.

# Technology Contributions

**Prof. Reggie:** As we noted, great economic advances were achieved through technology. But the GDP is a status quo measure. It does not reflect the gains from technologies that create entirely new goods and services.

**Stu:** You are saying the GDP measures contemporary economic variations.

**Prof. Reggie:** That's the general idea.

**Stu:** I'm not sure I get that.

**Prof. Reggie:** For example, the GDP counts postage as a cost of communicating by mail. On the other hand there is no incremental cost when sending an email. E-mail is the more productive way to communicate; yet that shows no contribution to the GDP, while postage does.

**Stu:** Putting it all together, you are saying: one - the GDP gives too much credit to government purchases; two - it treats the costs of regulations as pluses while they are actually negatives; three - it misses the economic benefits of technology advances.

**Prof. Reggie:** Quite so. That is a succinct recapitulation.

**Stu:** What then are the consequences of these GDP shortcomings, Professor?

**Prof. Reggie:** The GDP is commonly used to determine or support national economic policies. Policies that increase the GDP are favored – such as federal stimulus spending. These shortcomings of the GDP result in miss-directed economic policies.

**Stu:** Like booze. You get a quick buzz then a depression and a hangover.

**Prof. Reggie:** A hangover doesn't come close to the damage caused by stimulus spending.

## 4. STATE OF THE ECONOMY

**Prof. Reggie:** We identified sources of wealth and prosperity; and briefly discussed the pivotal role of government. We have seen that the GDP has serious flaws that lead to poor policy choices. Consequently for nearly a decade the economy has stalled.

Here is the GDP record for the last 20 years compared to median household income.

### CHART 1

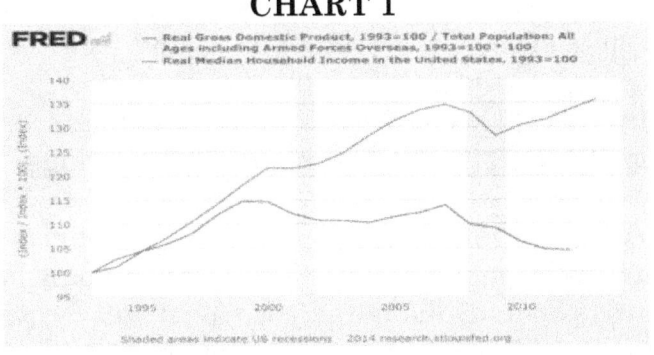

**Prof. Reggie:** As you see, the GDP grew at a healthy rate until 2007 when the real estate market collapsed. A massive government stimulus deficit spending brought the GDP back to the 2007 level.

**Prof. Reggie:**  Meanwhile the household income index declined nearly 10% from 115 to 105. Median income took a huge hit, declining from $56,000 in 2007 to $52,000.

**Stu:**  Incomes are hurting while your Keynesian economists say "keep on spending and everything will be ok."

**Prof. Reggie:**  Yes they do.  But the real world keeps miss-behaving.

**Stu:**  How so?

**Prof. Reggie:**  We had massive government stimulus spending . . . trillions of dollars . . . and in spite of the GDP it didn't do us any good.

**Stu:**  Recently I saw a headline "Job Market Ripe for Liftoff."  Something must be working.

**Prof. Reggie:**  That's a speculative headline; but lets' hope it happens.  The U. S. economy has always been resilient and perhaps it will recover in spite of heavy-handed government.

**Stu:**  We have an accumulated $18 trillion debt and counting, and an economy too weak to pay it off.

**Prof. Reggie:** Correct. That $18 trillion equals about $58,500 per person.

**Stu**: How depressing. I thought my net worth was about $4,000. Now you tell me it is minus $54,500.

**Prof. Reggie:** The national debt is a balance sheet item. To put it in perspective let's compare it to the national wealth, represented here as the sum of fixed assets and durable goods.

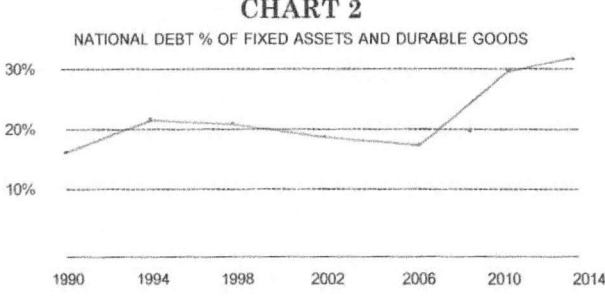

**CHART 2**

NATIONAL DEBT % OF FIXED ASSETS AND DURABLE GOODS

**Prof. Reggie:** For at least 20 years the debt was below 21%. That changed in 2008 when it accelerated to 30% and above.

**Stu:** Why?

**Prof. Reggie:** The rapid run-up in the national debt was triggered by the collapse of the housing market, which reduced the nation's housing assets.

**Prof. Reggie:**  Then the debt was further fueled by massive government deficit spending, labeled as "stimulus".

The nation's economy simply could not compensate for these two huge balance sheet losses.  For six years now the Federal Government has been consuming the nation's wealth.

## 5.  DESTROYERS

**Stu:**  Professor, as you pointed out we have a weak economy and a massive debt with no visible way to pay it off.  On, top of that, good jobs are scarce.  You said we would learn what policies are needed to promote growth.  So, what are they?

**Prof. Reggie:**  If we correctly identify the policies that stymie economic growth, the cures will be quite apparent.  They are not revolutionary and they are widely acknowledged.

**Stu:**  If they are widely acknowledged, why don't we just do them?

**Prof. Reggie:**  That's a fair question.  Perhaps there are some subtle reasons, but the obvious one is that for some people economic advancement is not a high priority.

**Stu:**  Must be nice to be rich!  What are their priorities?

**Prof. Reggie:**  We are not going there.  We are going to stay focused on economics.  Here are my Big Six Economic Destroyers.

## Destroyer #1:  Excessive Regulations

**Prof. Reggie:**  Government policies impose huge regulatory costs on the production of goods and services.  Mostly these are policies that do not yield value anywhere near their costs.  They are found everywhere regulatory agencies have law-making powers.

As of the end of 2014, federal regulations have grown to a cost of $1.86 trillion a year, larger than the economies of all but the ten largest countries.

**Stu:**  You say regulations do not provide economic benefits equal to their costs.  Can you back that up?

**Prof. Reggie**:  Yes.  Here is a prime example of regulatory overkill.  In the later 1990's to 2007, the U. S. real estate market became dominated by zero or low down payment loans guaranteed by Fannie Mae and Freddie Mac, government-backed real estate financing firms.  The Department of Housing and Urban Development promoted these ambitious affordable-housing goals that could only be achieved through lax underwriting.  Of course there was a boom in housing construction.

**Prof. Reggie**: In 2007, over-supply softened real estate values and mortgage defaults accelerated.  Fannie and Freddie became insolvent.  All of this is laid out in detail in the book "Hidden in Plain Sight" by Peter Wallison.

Subsequently a Financial Crisis Inquiry Commission asserted that banks and "Wall Street" were responsible.

In time, the narrative that banks were at fault became the basis for the Dodd-Frank Act.  Now we have arguably the most oppressive regulatory regime ever imposed on the U. S. economy; and it was built upon a false premise.

**Stu:**  Government housing policies caused the crisis; then they blamed it all on commercial and investment banks.  So what happens to the economy?

**Prof. Reggie:**  Having been justified on a false pretense, there can be no positive consequences – at least none that might have been intended.  On the other hand, there are massive compliance costs that impact negatively on the economy.

**Stu:**  That sounds like the patient nearly died from the prescription.

**Prof. Reggie:** Certainly the illness was miss-diagnosed. The patient is alive but poorer as he continues to pay the massive costs of Dodd-Frank regulations.
All of this is the result of what the Wall Street Journal called "The Fannie Mae Mortgage Fairy Tale".

Regulations are the means by which federal agencies exercise power and impose constraints on the economy. There is no remedy short of Congress reasserting its constitutional role.

**Stu:** That's pretty scary. What is the worst case?

**Prof. Reggie:** That freedom and private enterprise become history. Hark what Philip Hamburger, Professor Columbia Law School said:

> Those who forget history, it is often said, are doomed to repeat it. And this is what has happened in the United States with the rise of administrative law – or more accurately administrative power.

Regulatory reform must be job number one; all other remedial actions lag far behind.

**Stu:** Let's get going. Anti-regulation is the new look. Save us from ourselves.

**Prof. Reggie:** Here is an expeditious way to escape federal command and control.

> **Suspend all regulatory actions for five years.**

**Stu:** . . . That's it?

**Prof. Reggie:** Yes, that should do it quite nicely.

Of course Congress must proceed apace to reassert its authority over the laws of the land.

**Stu:** You are optimistic.

**Prof. Reggie:** Not so much optimistic as certain that if Congress can find the will to reverse the executive command and control model, the people will get the economy accelerating again.

**Stu:** That's cool. Let's do it.

**Prof. Reggie:** If Congress does not come to grips with this problem, then expanding federal command and control surely will in time destroy free enterprise.

**Stu:** Destroy free enterprise? That's like . . . doomsday! Professor, you can't be serious?

**Prof. Reggie:** As the executive branch becomes omnipotent, Congress becomes irrelevant. Yes, that really is serious.

## Destroyed #2: Fossil Fuel Abandonment

**Prof. Reggie:** Supposedly $CO_2$ emissions are the cause of global warming. Unchecked, $CO_2$ emissions will warm the globe to the point where polar ice caps melt and seas rise. One hundred years or so from now we will experience world-wide flooding – that is according to the global warming mathematical model. This doomsday scenario is not a serious threat; the science is flawed. (Ed: See "A COOL EXPERIENCE" an earlier Astro Science essay.)

**Stu:** What if you are wrong?

**Prof. Reggie:** Not a chance. But even if you discount my conclusion, a five-year hiatus on writing regulations is a no risk, all win proposition, because fossil fuels have a huge economic edge over any energy alternative.

### Destroyer #3: Affordable Care Act

**Prof. Reggie:**  Another major economic depressor is the Affordable Care Act (ACA).  The ACA contains huge economic disincentives – penalties on full time jobs; penalties for adding employees; penalties just for working.

**Stu:**  I think I get your drift.  Regulations slowly suffocate us while the ACA is more like a cardiac arrest.

**Prof. Reggie:**  Choose your poison - economic decline, fast or slow.

# Destroyer #4: Uncompetitive Corporate Taxes

**Prof. Reggie:** Now we have corporate taxes driving businesses out of the country. The process is commonly referred to as inversions.

**Stu:** U. S. corporations move overseas to reduce taxes.

**Prof. Reggie:** They are orchestrating their own takeovers by foreign companies. A U. S. company arranges to have a foreign company buy its operations. Assets are then owned by the foreign company, and the old company is dissolved. Being now incorporated abroad, the company avoids higher U.S. taxes on income that is not generated in the United States.

**Stu:** Isn't that kind of shady?

**Prof. Reggie:** Not at all. Corporations have obligations to their shareholders to be profitable and to return adequate dividends. Maximizing profits is not immoral; it is a crucial feature of free enterprise and a dynamic economy.

# Destroyer #5: Minimum Wage Laws

**Prof. Reggie:** If the minimum wage is say $8 an hour and small businesses are able to achieve satisfactory returns on their investments, then we might conclude that minimum wages are effective and not harmful for the economy.

**Stu:** Success validates the principle.

**Prof. Reggie:** Exactly. It is an easy step in logic to say that a minimum wage of say $12 would be even better for workers and the economy. After all, you can't support a family on $8 an hour.

**Stu:** I see where you are going.

**Prof. Reggie:** Good. Please continue.

**Stu:** If a business is selling burgers, it would have to raise prices from $2 to say $3 to pay $12 per hour wages. And maybe their customers would not pay that price; they go somewhere else or eat at home more often.

**Prof. Reggie:** When wages are forced higher than the market can accommodate, something has to give. In this instance business models that depend on low wages fail.

**Prof. Reggie:** This scenario is not hypothetical. There are multiple examples around the country where businesses have failed as a result of minimum wage increases. For example, according to a Chamber of Commerce member in Oakland California ten restaurants and grocery stores closed in 2014 due to minimum wage hikes.

The rest, as they say, is history. Businesses decline; workers are laid off; the economy suffers.

## Destroyer # 6: Deficit Spending

**Prof. Reggie:** We have discussed how deficit spending drains capital out of the economy. The obvious solution is to balance the budget and stop the bleeding.

**Stu:** But that still leaves us with an $18 trillion debt.

**Prof. Reggie:** We have a small ray of hope. If we balance the budget, the deficit will stop growing. If we also get the economy moving forward the deficit will gradually diminish in both relative and absolute terms.

**Stu:** That's two very large ifs.

**Prof. Reggie:** To be sure, our entire wish list is iffy. The backup plan is that you are going to become missionaries.

**Stu:** Professor Reggie, do you feel ok?

**Prof. Reggie:** Quite well, thank you.

**Stu:** I'm afraid you lost us with this missionary notion.

## 6. THE MISSION

**Prof. Reggie:** Let's review some basics. Liberty is indivisible; political freedom cannot exist without economic freedom. The purpose of government is to protect these freedoms through the preservation of internal order, the provision of national defense, and the administration of justice.

When government ventures beyond these basics, it accumulates power and diminishes liberty and private enterprise.

**Stu:** Don't regulations preserve internal order?

**Prof. Reggie:** That's a bit of a stretch. Internal order refers to public safety and protection of property.

Our Constitution empowers government to fulfill its role while restraining it from abusing that power.

**Stu:** Many people say the Constitution is archaic and needs interpreted for the modern world.

**Prof. Reggie:** Who gets to be the interpreter?

**Stu:** The Supreme Court, I guess. Who else?

**Prof. Reggie:** Who else indeed. How quickly we forget. The Constitution empowers the people and only the people to modify it. Neither the Supreme Court nor the President nor the Congress is empowered to do that.

**Stu:** That's all well and good. So?

**Prof. Reggie:** As I said, the Constitution empowers the people and only the people. You are the people. You cannot pass the buck. Senators and Representatives are all yours.

**Stu:** Whoa – back up a minute. We're here to learn basic economics and earn a Bachelor of Science degree, not to be missionaries.

**Stu:** We're not going out and preach about how Congress is failing to do its job? No way.

**Prof. Reggie:** It is too late to protest. You cannot deny your knowledge; and with that comes responsibility. So now you may not turn your back as science is abused and your fellow citizens are led astray with half-truths and biased agendas.

Go and do your duty. Class is dismissed.

Stu: Aw gee . . .

**Prof. Reggie:** You have my sympathy.

(Ed: Professor Regina Worthy exits the classroom smiling.)

END

# Handout A
# Suggested Readings

**The Failure of Macroeconomics** by John Cochrane - Wall Street Journal, July 3, 2014.

**The Road to Serfdom** by Friedrich Hayck - Heritage Foundation.

**Zero to One** by Peter Thiel - Silicon Valley Venture Capitalist.

**One Nation Under Arrest** by Paul Rosenzwieg & Brian Welch - Heritage Foundation.

**Hidden in Plain Sight** by Peter J. Wallison.

# About the Author

John S. Thomas was Deputy Director of the Budget, City of New York during the second John Lindsay mayoral term.  There he directed a city-wide productivity improvement program that achieved national acclaim.

Subsequently he wrote "So, Mr. Mayor, You Want to Improve Productivity . . ." published by the National Commission on Productivity and Work Quality in cooperation with the Ford Foundation.

Mr. Thomas also wrote "A Cool Experience", an essay about climate science and a companion to "A Worthy Experience".

Mr. Thomas has extensive management consulting experience with major U. S. industrial and financial companies and the Department of Defense.  He is a graduate of the University of Pennsylvania, Towne School of Engineering.